# Van Dyck

A Collection of Fifteen Pictures and a Portrait of the
Painter with Introduction and Interpretation

Estelle M. Hurll

**Alpha Editions**

This edition published in 2024

ISBN : 9789362926371

Design and Setting By
**Alpha Editions**
www.alphaedis.com
Email - info@alphaedis.com

As per information held with us this book is in Public Domain.
This book is a reproduction of an important historical work. Alpha Editions uses the best technology to reproduce historical work in the same manner it was first published to preserve its original nature. Any marks or number seen are left intentionally to preserve its true form.

# Contents

PREFACE ........................................................................... - 1 -
INTRODUCTION ............................................................ - 2 -
I ......................................................................................... - 11 -
II ........................................................................................ - 14 -
III ....................................................................................... - 17 -
IV ...................................................................................... - 20 -
V ........................................................................................ - 23 -
VI ...................................................................................... - 26 -
VII ..................................................................................... - 29 -
VIII .................................................................................... - 32 -
IX ...................................................................................... - 35 -
X ........................................................................................ - 38 -
XI ...................................................................................... - 41 -
XII ..................................................................................... - 44 -
XIII .................................................................................... - 47 -
XIV .................................................................................... - 50 -
XV ..................................................................................... - 53 -
XVI .................................................................................... - 56 -

# PREFACE

The fame of Van Dyck's portraits has so far over-shadowed that of his other works that his sacred pictures are for the most part unfamiliar to the general public. The illustrations for this little book are equally divided between portraits and subject-pieces, and it is hoped that the selection may give the reader some adequate notion of the scope of the painter's art.

ESTELLE M. HURLL.

NEW BEDFORD, MASS.,

March, 1902.

# INTRODUCTION

## I. ON VAN DYCK'S CHARACTER AS AN ARTIST.

The student of Van Dyck's art naturally classifies the painter's works into four groups, corresponding chronologically to the four successive periods of his life. There was first the short period of his youth in Antwerp, when Rubens was the dominating influence upon his work. The portrait of Van der Geest, in the National Gallery, belongs to this time.

Then followed the four years' residence in Italy, when he fell under the spell of Titian. This was the period of the series of splendid portraits of noble Italian families which are to this day the pride of Genoa. Here too belong those lovely Madonna pictures which brought back for a time the golden age of Venetian art.

Upon his return to Antwerp, the six succeeding years gave him the opportunity to work out his own individuality. Some noble altar-pieces were produced in these years. Pleasant reminiscences of Titian still appear in such work, as in the often-used motif of baby angels; but in the subjects of the Crucifixion and the Pietà, he stands quite apart. These works are distinctly his own, and show genuine dramatic power.

During this Flemish period Van Dyck was appointed court painter by the Archduchess Isabella Clara Eugenia, Spanish Regent of the Netherlands. In this capacity he painted a notable series of portraits, including some of his most interesting works, which represent many of the most distinguished personages of the time.

The last nine years of Van Dyck's life were passed in England, where the family of Charles I. and the brilliant group of persons forming his court were the subjects of his final series of portraits. There were no altar-pieces in this period. At the beginning of his English work Van Dyck produced certain portraits unsurpassed during his whole life. The well-known Charles I., with an equerry, in the Louvre, is perhaps the best of these. His works after this were uneven in quality. His vitality was drained by social dissipations, and he lost the ambition to grow. Some features of the portraits became stereotyped, especially the hands. Yet from time to time he rose to a high level.

A painter so easily moulded by his environment cannot justly take rank among the world's foremost masters. A great creative mind Van Dyck certainly had not, but, gifted assimilator that he was, he developed many delightful qualities of his art. The combined results of his borrowing and his own innate gifts make him a notable and indeed a beloved figure in art history.

The leading note of his style is distinction. His men are all noblemen, his women all great ladies, and his children all princes and princesses. The same qualities of dignity and impressiveness are carried into his best altar-pieces. Sentiment they have also in no insignificant degree.

It is perhaps naming only another phase of distinction to say that his figures are usually characterized by repose. The sense of motion which so many of Reynolds's portraits convey is almost never expressed in Van Dyck's work, nor would it be consistent with his other qualities.

The magic gift of charm none have understood better when the subject offered the proper inspiration. We see this well illustrated in many portraits of young noblemen, such as the Duke of Lennox and Richmond and Lord Wharton.

Van Dyck's clever technique has preserved for us the many rich fabrics of his period, and his pictures would be a delight were these details their sole attraction. Heavy velvet, with the light playing deliciously in the creases, lustrous satins, broken by folds into many tints, delicate laces, elaborate embroideries, gleaming jewels—these are the never-failing accessories of his compositions. Yet while he loved rich draperies, he was also a careful student of the nude. Examples of his work range from the supple and youthful torso of Icarus to the huge muscular body of the beggar receiving St. Martin's cloak. The modelling of the Saviour's body in the Crucifixion and the Pietà shows both scientific knowledge and artistic handling.

Generally speaking, Van Dyck was little of a psychologist. His patrons belonged to that social class in which reserve is a test of breeding and thoughts and emotions are sedulously concealed. To penetrate the mask of the face and interpret the character of his sitter was an office he seldom took upon himself to perform. Yet he was capable of profound character study, especially in the portrayal of men. Even in so early a work as the so-called portrait of Richardot and his son, he revealed decided talent in this direction, while the portrait of Cardinal Bentivoglio, of the Italian period, and the portrait of Wentworth, in the English period, are masterly studies of the men they represent.

A common feature of his portraits is the averted glance of the sitter's eyes. This fact is in itself a barrier to our intimate knowledge of the subject, and also in a measure injures the sense of vitality expressed in the work. It must be confessed that Van Dyck, disciple though he was of Rubens and Titian, fell below these masters in the art of imparting life to a figure.

In certain mechanical elements of his art Van Dyck was conspicuously deficient. He seemed to have no ingenuity in devising poses for his subjects. Sitting or standing, the attitude is usually more or less artificial and constrained. The atmosphere of the studio is painfully evident. Never by any accident did he seem to catch the sitter off guard, so to speak, except in a few children's portraits. Here he expressed a vivacity and charm which seemed impossible to him with adult subjects.

In composition he is at his best in altar-pieces. In portrait groups, as in the pictures of the children of Charles I., he apparently made no effort to bring the separate figures into an harmonious unity. A single figure, or half length, he placed on his canvas with unerring sense of right proportion. Perhaps the best summary of Van Dyck's art has been made by the English critic, Claude Phillips, in these words: His was "not indeed one of the greatest creative individualities that have dominated the world of art, but a talent as exquisite in distinction, as true to itself in every successive phase, a technical accomplishment as surprising of its kind in solidity, brilliancy, and charm, as any that could be pointed to even in the seventeenth century."

## II. ON BOOKS OF REFERENCE.

It has been reserved for our own day to produce two superb works by English writers on Van Dyck. The first to appear was that by Ernest Law, "a storehouse of information," on the paintings by Van Dyck in the Royal Collections. The second is the definitive biography by Lionel Cust: "Anthony Van Dyck; An Historical Study of his Life and Works." The author is the director of the English National Portrait Gallery, and has had exceptional opportunities for the examination of Van Dyck's paintings. His work has been done with great thoroughness and care. The volume is richly illustrated with photogravures, and contains complete lists of the painter's works arranged by periods.

For brief sketches of Van Dyck's life the student is referred to general histories, of which Kugler's "Hand-book of the German, Flemish, and Dutch School" (revised by Crowe), is of first importance. Lübke's "History of Painting," and Woltman and Woerman's "History of Painting," contain material on Van Dyck. A volume devoted to Van Dyck is in the series of German monographs edited by H. Knackfuss, and may be had in an English translation.

A critical appreciation of Van Dyck is given by Fromentin in his valuable little book on "The Old Masters of Holland and Belgium." Critical articles by Claude Phillips have appeared in "The Nineteenth Century," November, 1899, and "The Art Journal" for March, 1900.

## III. HISTORICAL DIRECTORY OF THE PICTURES OF THIS COLLECTION.

Frontispiece. *Portrait of Van Dyck*. Detail of a portrait of Van Dyck and John Digby, Earl of Bristol. Painted about 1640. Formerly in the Isabel Farnese

Collection in the palace of San Ildefonso; now in the Prado Gallery, Madrid. *Cust*, p. 285.

1. *Portrait of Anna Wake*, inscribed: "Ætat suæ 22, An 1628." Signed: "Anton Van Dyck fecit." In the Royal Gallery at the Hague. Size: 3 ft. 8-1/2 in. by 3 ft. 2-1/2 in. *Cust*, pp. 58 and 261.

2. *The Rest in Egypt*. Painted in the Italian period for Frederick Henry, Prince of Orange. One of several pictures of the same subject, and generally considered the original, though the authenticity is doubted by Signor Venturi. In the Pitti, Florence.

3. *The so-called Portrait of Richardot and his Son*. The identity of the subject not established. Sometimes attributed to Rubens, but accepted as Van Dyck's work by Cust. In the Louvre, Paris. Size: 3 ft. 7 in. by 2 ft. 5-1/2 in. *Cust*, pp. 76 and 134.

4. *The Vision of St. Anthony*. Painted in the Italian period. Obtained by exchange in 1813 from the Musée National at Paris. In the Brera Gallery, Milan. Size: 6 ft. 1 in. by 5 ft. 1/4 in. *Cust*, pp. 46 and 239.

5. *Madame Andreas Colyns de Nole and her Daughter*. Painted in Antwerp in period from 1626 to 1632. Purchased in 1698 by the Elector Max Emanuel of Bavaria. Munich Gallery. Size: 3 ft. 11-1/2 in. by 2 ft. 11-2/5 in. *Cust*, pp. 79 and 254.

6. *Dædalus and Icarus*. Painted about 1621 (?). Exhibited at Antwerp in 1899. One of several paintings of the same subject. In the collection of the Earl of Spencer, Althorp. *Cust*, pp. 61 and 241.

7. *Portrait of Charles I*. Supposed to be a copy by Sir Peter Lely from the original, which was painted about 1636, and destroyed in the fire at Whitehall in 1697. Not impossibly, however, the original painting itself, given by the king to the Prince Palatine. In the Dresden Gallery. Size: 4 ft. by 3 ft. 2 in. *Cust*, pp. 105 and 264.

8. *The Madonna of St. Rosalia*. Painted in 1629 for the Confraternity of Celibates in the Hall of the Jesuits, Antwerp. On the suppression of the order in 1776 it was purchased by the Empress Maria Theresa. Now in the Imperial Gallery, Vienna. Size: 9 ft. 1 in. by 6 ft. 11 in. *Cust*, p. 250.

9. *Charles, Prince of Wales*. Detail of a group of the three children of Charles I., painted in 1635. Probably painted for the queen, and presented by her to her sister Christina of Savoy. In the Royal Gallery, Turin. *Cust*, pp. 110 and 266.

10. *St. Martin dividing his Cloak with a Beggar*. Painted in the Italian period. Presented to the Church of Saventhem by Ferdinand de Boisschot, Seigneur de Saventhem. Taken by the French to Paris in 1806 and returned in 1815.

A copy of this picture is in the Imperial Gallery, Vienna, but the original is in the church of Saventhem. *Cust*, pp. 32 and 240.

11. *The Crucifixion*. Painted in 1628 for the church of St. Augustine at Antwerp. Taken by the French to Paris in 1794 and restored in 1815. Now in the Antwerp Museum. Size: 3 ft. 5 in. by 2 ft. 4 in. *Cust*, pp. 61 and 248.

12. *James Stuart, Duke of Lennox and Richmond.* Painted about 1633. Formerly belonged to Lord Methuen at Corsham. Now in the Marquand collection at the Metropolitan Art Museum, New York. Size: 4 ft. 3/4 in. by 6 ft. 11-5/8 in. *Cust*, pp. 117-278.

13. *Christ and the Paralytic. Painted at Genoa.* In Buckingham Palace. Size: 3 ft. 10-1/2 in. by 4 ft. 9 in. *Cust*, pp. 46 and 237.

14. *Philip, Lord Wharton*. Inscribed in the lower left corner with the painter's name; in the lower right corner, "Philip, Lord Wharton, 1632, about y$^e$ age of 19." Purchased from the Duke of Wharton's collection in 1725 by Sir Robert Walpole, and thence it passed in 1779 to the collection of Catherine II. of Russia. In the Hermitage Gallery, St. Petersburg. Size: 4 ft. 5 in. by 2 ft. 4 in. *Cust*, pp. 121 and 286.

15. *The Lamentation over Christ.* Painted about 1629 for the church of the Béguinage at Antwerp. Now in the Antwerp Museum. Size: 9 ft. 11 in. by 7 ft. 4 in. *Cust*, pp. 66 and 248.

## IV. OUTLINE TABLE OF THE PRINCIPAL EVENTS IN VAN DYCK'S LIFE.

*Compiled from Lionel Cust's* **Anthony Van Dyck**, *to which the references to pages apply.*

1599. Antoon Van Dyck born March 22, in the house "der Berendaus," Antwerp (p. 4).

1601. Removal of Van Dyck family to house number 46 in street De Stat Gent (p. 4).

1607. Death of Van Dyck's mother (p. 4).

1609. Van Dyck among the apprentices of the painter Hendrick van Balen (p. 6).

1613. Portrait of an old man (p. 7).

1618. Admitted to the freedom of the Guild of St. Luke, Antwerp, February (p. 8). Entered Rubens' studio (p. 15).

1620. An order from the Jesuits for thirty-nine pictures designed by Rubens and completed by Van Dyck (p. 14).

Visit to England and service for King James I. (p. 23), and return to Antwerp (p. 24).

1621. Departure for Italy, Oct. 3 (p. 25), arriving at Genoa, Nov. 21.

1622. Departure from Genoa, February, to Rome; thence to Florence (p. 26); thence to Bologna (p. 27); thence to Venice (p. 27); Mantua (p. 27). Death of Van Dyck's father, Dec. 1 (p. 55).

1623. Return to Rome (p. 27); thence to Genoa (p. 28).

1623-1625. In Genoa.

1624. Journey to Palermo for portraits and other pictures (p. 49).

1625. Crucifixion, with St. Francis, St. Bernard, and the donor, painted for church of S. Michele de Pagana, near Genoa (p. 48).

1626. Probable date of return to Antwerp (p. 55).

1626 or 1627. Probable visit to England (pp. 56, 57, and 85).

1627. Death of Van Dyck's sister Cornelia (p. 58).

1628, March 3. Date of Van Dyck's will (p. 58).

1628. St. Augustine in Ecstasy completed for church of St. Augustine, Antwerp (p. 61).

1629. Purchase of Rinaldo and Armida by Charles I. (p. 85).

1630. Crucifixion for church of St. Michel, Ghent (p. 63). Portrait of Anna Maria de Camudio, wife of Ferdinand de Boisschot (p. 75).

1631. Elevation of Cross for church of Notre Dame at Courtray (p. 64). Appointment as court painter to Isabella Clara Eugenia, regent of the Netherlands (p. 73).

1630, 1631. Portraits of Philippe le Roy, Seigneur de Ravels and his wife (p. 78).

1631. Portrait of Marie de Medici (p. 81).

1631? Visit to Holland and acquaintance with Franz Hals (pp. 81-83).

1632. Arrival in England (p. 87), and knighthood conferred, July 5 (p. 88).

1634. Double portrait of Charles I. and Henrietta Maria (p. 102). Visit to Antwerp and purchase of property there (p. 90). Visit to Court of Brussels and portraits of regent, Prince of Savoy, and Prince Gaston, duc d'Orléans, and others (p. 91).

1635. Return to Antwerp, thence to England (p. 96). Famous portrait of Charles I. with horse and equerry (now in Louvre), sent to France as gift to queen mother (p. 105). Group of three children of Charles I., now in Turin (p. 109). 1636. Portrait of Charles I., full length, at Windsor Castle (p. 105).

1637. Group of five children of Charles I. (p. 111).

1639 or 1640. Marriage with Mary Ruthven (p. 142).

1640. In Antwerp in October, magnificently entertained by Academy of Painting (p. 143).

1641. In Paris, in January, seeking commission for decorations of Louvre (p. 144). In London, in May, and portrait of Princess Mary and Prince William (p. 144). In Antwerp, in October, planning for residence there (p. 145). In Paris, in November, on business. Return to London. Birth of daughter, Dec. 1. Death, Dec. 9 (p. 145).

## V. LIST OF CONTEMPORARY PAINTERS.

*Flemish:—*

- Franz Snyders, 1579-1657.
- Peter Paul Rubens, 1577-1640.
- Gaspard de Craeyer, 1582-1669.
- Jacob Jordaens, 1594-1678.
- Justus Sustermans, 1597-1681.
- David Teniers, 1610-1690.

*Spanish:—*

- Pacheco, 1571-1654.
- Herrera, 1576-1656.
- Zurbaran, 1598-1662.
- Velasquez, 1599-1660.
- Cano, 1601-1676.
- Murillo, 1618-1682.

*French:—*

- Simon Vouet, 1582-1641.
- Poussin, 1594-1655. Eustache Le Sueur, 1617-1655.

- Charles Le Brun, 1619-1690.

*Italian:—*

- Guido Reni, 1575-1642.
- Francesco Albani, 1578-1660.
- Domenichino, 1581-1641.
- Guercino, 1591-1666.
- Sassoferrato, 1605-1685.
- Carlo Dolci, 1616-1686.

*Dutch:—*

- Franz Hals, 1584-1666.
- Gerard Honthorst, 1590-1656.
- Jan van Goypen, 1596-1656.
- Albert Cuyp, 1605-1691.
- Rembrandt, 1606-1669.
- Jan Lievens, 1607-after 1672.
- Gerard Terburg, 1608-1681.
- Salomon Koning, 1609-1668.
- Adrian van Ostade, 1610-1685.

## VI. NOTABLE ENGLISH PERSONS OF THE REIGN OF CHARLES I.

*Writers:—*

- Ben Jonson, 1573 or 1574-1637.
- Robert Herrick, 1591-1674.
- George Herbert, 1593-1632.
- Edmund Waller, 1605 or 1606-1687.
- Sir William Killigrew, 1605-1693.
- Sir John Suckling, 1608 or 1609-1641 or 1642.
- John Milton, 1608-1674.
- Thomas Killigrew, 1611-1682.

- John Evelyn, 1620-1706 (author of "Memoirs").

*Architect.—*

- Inigo Jones, 1572-1653.

*Royalists:—*

- Archbishop Laud, 1573-1644/5.
- Thomas Howard, Earl of Arundel, 1586-1646.
- George Villiers, first Duke of Buckingham, 1592-1628.
- Thomas Wentworth, Earl of Strafford, 1593-1641.

*Parliamentarians:—*

- John Pym, 1584-1643.
- Sir John Eliot, 1592-1632.
- John Hampden, 1594-1643.
- Oliver Cromwell, 1599-1658.
- Lord Thomas Fairfax, 1611 or 1612-1671.

# I

## PORTRAIT OF ANNA WAKE

The city of Antwerp was at one time famous for its commercial and industrial interests, and it was besides an important centre of art. Here in the seventeenth century lived the two foremost Flemish painters, Peter Paul Rubens, and Anthony Van Dyck. The Flemish industries had chiefly to do with the making of beautiful things. Among them were tapestries in rich designs and many colors, used for wall hangings. The Flemish weavers were also skilled in making fabrics of silk and velvet. Most famous of all were their laces, patiently wrought by hand, on pillows, and unrivalled throughout the world for delicacy of workmanship. Glass and porcelain were also among their industrial products. In Antwerp, too, was the printing establishment of Plantin, from which issued many learned works in French and Latin.

Among refined people like these, who not only loved beautiful things but could afford to buy them, the art of painting was highly esteemed. There was every encouragement for a young artist to pursue this calling. Rubens was already a great painter when Van Dyck began his art studies, and the older man gave the younger much helpful advice. At his friend's suggestion Van Dyck travelled several years in Italy, where he was inspired by the works of the Italian masters of the preceding century. Returning at length to his native city, he set up a studio of his own, and soon became a favorite portrait painter among the rich and fashionable classes. Not a few of his sitters were foreign sojourners in the Netherlands, especially the English. The lady of our illustration is quite plainly of this nationality, though she is dressed according to the Flemish modes.

It appears that an English merchant named Wake was established in Antwerp at this time, and it is supposed that this may be his daughter. There are also reasons for connecting the portrait with one of a certain English baronet named Sheffield, who was likewise in Belgium in this period. Miss Anna Wake, we may conclude, had married into the Sheffield family when this portrait was painted. These names, however, are mere guesses, and, even if they were verified, would tell us no more of the lady's story than we can gather from the picture. Her life was probably not of the eventful kind which passes into history. The luxuries of her surroundings we may judge from her rich dress and jewels; the sweetness of her character is written in her face.

She shows us perhaps more of her inner life than she intends. Her fine reserve would naturally shrink from any sort of familiarity. Yet as she stands quietly before the portrait painter, left, as it were, to the solitude of her own thoughts, her spirit seems to look out of the candid eyes.

**PORTRAIT OF ANNA WAKE**
Royal Gallery, The Hague

Her dignity and self-possession make her seem older than the twenty-two years with which the inscription on the portrait credits her. But the face is that of one who has just passed from maidenhood to young womanhood. Life lies before her, and with sweet seriousness she builds her air castles of the future. Thus far she has been carefully guarded from the evil of the world, and her heart is as pure as that of "the lily maid of Astolat." For social triumphs she would care nothing, though her beauty could not fail to draw an admiring throng about her. Vanity and coquetry are altogether foreign to her nature. She is, rather, of a poetic and dreamy temperament. Perhaps it is the fragile quality of her beauty which gives an almost wistful expression to the face. She is like a delicate flower which a chill wind would blast.

The costume interests us as a study of bygone fashions, and is painted with exquisite care for detail. The pointed bodice is as stiff as a coat of mail, like that so long in vogue at the court of Spain. Perhaps the Spanish occupation of the Netherlands may have brought the corset with it. Certainly it is not conducive to an easy carriage; only a graceful figure like this could wear it without awkwardness. The slashed sleeves are made full, and tied at the elbows with bows. The wide collar and cuffs are edged with beautiful Flemish lace points. The feather fan and the strings of pearls about the throat and wrists might form a part of any modern costume. It strikes us, however, as a very singular fashion for a lady to wear a large seal ring on the thumb.

We notice how simply the hair is dressed, brushed loosely from the face and knotted at the back, with a jewel gleaming at one side. Compared with the elaborate coiffures worn by great ladies in some historical periods, this style is delightfully artistic. Altogether the entire manner of dressing is perfectly suited to the wearer.

# II

## THE REST IN EGYPT

We often read in history of the rejoicing throughout a kingdom over the birth of a prince: messengers are sent from place to place to proclaim the glad news, congratulations and gifts follow, every possible care is taken for the nurture and protection of the precious young life.

The story of the childhood of Jesus reads somewhat like that of a prince, in spite of his lowly surroundings. Though he was born in a manger, a herald angel announced the glad tidings of his coming. Though the people of Bethlehem took no note of the event, a multitude of the heavenly host sang "Glory to God in the highest, on earth peace, good-will to men." Wise men from the East made a long journey to find the young child. The lore of the stars had taught them that he was a king, and they brought gifts worthy of royalty, gold, and frankincense, and myrrh.

It was these visitors who were the innocent cause of the child's first danger. In seeking him out they had gone to King Herod at Jerusalem, asking, "Where is he that is born King of the Jews?" These inquiries made the monarch very uneasy. He had no mind to lose his crown. To prevent the appearance of any possible rival he determined upon summary measures. "He sent forth and slew all the children that were in Bethlehem, and in all the coasts thereof, from two years old and under." By this terrible massacre he thought to do away with the child Jesus.

But the Prince of Peace was protected by stronger guards than ever surrounded the cradle of an earthly prince. A warning message was sent to save the child from the impending danger. "The angel of the Lord appeareth to Joseph in a dream, saying, Arise, and take the young child and his mother, and flee into Egypt, and be thou there until I bring thee word: for Herod will seek the young child to destroy him."

"When he arose, he took the young child and his mother by night, and departed into Egypt."[1] The journey was long and wearisome, but the mother Mary was young, and strong in courage, and Joseph was a sturdy defender. As for the babe, what mattered it to him whether he slept in a manger, or under the trees by the wayside? He was safe in his mother's arms.

[1] St. Matthew, chapter ii., verses 13, 14.

What adventures befell them by the way we do not know, but we like to imagine the incidents of the journey. There is a tradition that angel playfellows came from time to time to amuse the child Jesus. When Mary and Joseph were forced to pause a little while for food and rest, the lonely places were filled with these glad presences.

**THE REST IN EGYPT**
**Pitti Gallery, Florence**

This is the legend illustrated in our picture. Under the spreading branches of a great tree, Mary has found a comfortable seat on a grassy bank, and Joseph rests behind her. The little child stands on his mother's knee, clinging to her dress for support, while her arms hold him firm. A band of infant angels play on the flower-strewn grass in the open space in front. With joined hands they circle about as in the figure of a dance or game. The music for their sport is furnished by a heavenly choir, hovering in the upper air and singing the score from an open book.

The leader of the dance is evidently the beautiful angel who pauses opposite the Christ-child. Resting on the right foot he draws back the left, poising on his toe, in an attitude of exquisite grace. With his left hand he waves a salute to the infant Christ. His right hand clasps that of a companion angel to form an arch beneath which troop the whole jocund company. It is good sport, and the players scamper gleefully along. A single angel stops to gaze ardently towards the Christ-child.

The mother looks on at the game with queenly dignity. A smile hovers on her lips, as if the eagerness of the little leader pleased her. As for Joseph, his glance is directed towards the tree-tops. Perhaps his senses are not fine enough to discern the spirit company, but he is well content with the happiness of mother and child.

From the safe pedestal of his mother's knee the child Jesus watches every motion of the angels with breathless interest. The angel leader seems to beckon him to join them, and he is almost ready to go. Yet the firm hands hold him back, and he is glad to cling to his mother's dress. A circle of light about his head is the halo, or symbol of his divine origin.

The picture is an important record of our painter's travels in Italy. It was here he imbibed from the old Italian masters the tender and devotional spirit which animated their sacred works. Titian was the special object of his admiration, and he painted a number of Madonna pictures which show the influence the Venetian painter had upon his art. The circle of dancing angels recalls the cherub throng of Titian's Assumption.[2]

[2] See Chapter XII. in volume on Titian in the Riverside Art Series.

# III

## THE SO-CALLED PORTRAIT OF RICHARDOT AND HIS SON

A gentleman has brought his little boy to our painter's studio for a portrait sitting. Father and son are close friends and understand each other well. On the way they have talked of the picture that is to be made, and the boy has asked many questions about it. It is rather a tedious prospect to an active child to have to sit still a long time. But his father's companionship is his greatest delight, and it is a rare treat to both to have a whole morning together. Besides, they have a book with them, a new publication from the Plantin printing press, and the father has promised to read something to him.

The two are richly dressed for the event, the father in black with a fur mantle, and the boy in white satin embroidered with gold. The man wears the stiff quilled ruff of the period, the boy a round collar of soft lace. It is not every day in the year that a little boy is allowed to wear his best satin doublet, and the child feels the gravity of the occasion. We may suppose that these are people of distinction, and that on certain great occasions the boy accompanies his father to court. Perhaps, too, as the eldest son of the house, he is sometimes given a seat at a great banquet, or is brought into the tapestried hall to meet an honored guest. It is at such times that he would be dressed as in the picture. In our own day a child's finery brings to mind dancing classes and parties, but in these far away times it is associated only with stately ceremonies.

The painter has led his guests to a place near a window, where, looking over their shoulders, one sees a bit of pleasant country. The man draws the boy towards him and lays one hand on the child's shoulder. At the painter's bidding, the little fellow puts his right arm akimbo, imitating the attitude in some of the portraits of the studio. The pose suits perfectly the quaint dignity of the little figure.

It is a proud moment for the boy. It makes him almost a man to be treated as an equal by his father. Not for worlds would he do anything to spoil the picture; he feels the responsibility of carrying out his part well. He regards the painter with solemn eyes, watching intently every motion of the pencil.

There is a gleam of humor in the father's eyes as he too looks in the same direction. He is a man of large affairs, we are sure. His high forehead shows rare mental powers, and he has the judicial expression of one whose counsel would be worth following. Yet there is that in his face which shows the quiet tastes of the scholar. With his boy beside him and a book in his hand, he is content to let the great world go its way. Nevertheless he is something of a courtier, as his station in life requires, a distinguished figure in any great company. The face is one of striking nobility of character. He is a man in whom we could place great confidence.

**THE SO-CALLED PORTRAIT OF RICHARDOT AND HIS SON**
The Louvre, Paris

Two qualities of the portrait give it artistic value, life-likeness, and character. The figures almost seem to speak to us from the canvas, and we feel a sense of intimacy with them, as if we had actually known them in real life. Indeed there is very little in the picture to make it seem foreign to our own surroundings. The stiff ruff is the most distinctly old-fashioned feature. The man's closely cut pointed beard is such as has long been called the "Van Dyck beard." The painter wore his own trimmed in the same way, which seems at one time to have been equally the fashion in England and on the continent.

We remark in the picture the excellent characterization of the hands. In later days when the painter was busier, he often assigned this part of the work to assistants. They did not try to reproduce the hand of the portrait sitter, but painted this feature from a model. Now this man's hand is plainly his own; it is of a character with the face, strong and sensitive.

The landscape view is an important element in the picture. If we compare our illustration with others which have no such setting, we shall better understand its value. An enclosed space sets a more or less definite limit to the imagination. A glimpse of the country, on the other hand, suggests wide spaces for the fancy to explore. It will also be noticed that this light spot in the upper right corner balances well the white costume of the boy in the lower left corner.

The portrait group of our illustration has long borne the title of Jean Grusset Richardot and his Son. This Richardot was a celebrated Flemish diplomat of the sixteenth century, and president of the Privy Council of the Low Countries. As he died in Van Dyck's boyhood, his portrait could not have been made by our painter directly from life. Nor can we believe with some that years after the diplomat's death Van Dyck copied from some old picture the likeness seen here. A portrait painted in this way would not have the vitality of our illustration. We are therefore obliged to consider the picture nameless; but our enjoyment of its good qualities is by no means less keen.

# IV

## THE VISION OF ST. ANTHONY

St. Anthony of Padua was a Franciscan friar of the thirteenth century, celebrated for his piety and eloquence. He was a Portuguese by birth, and early in life determined to be a Christian missionary. His first labors were in Africa, but being seized by a lingering illness, he returned to Europe and landed in Italy. Here he came under the influence of St. Francis of Assisi, who was just establishing a new religious order. The rules were to be very strict: the members could possess nothing of their own, but were to beg their food and raiment of fellow Christians. They were to mingle with the people as brothers, hence *friars*,[3] ministering to their bodily needs, and advising, comforting, and admonishing in higher concerns. What sort of a habit they wore we may see in our picture. There was a long dark brown tunic made with loose sleeves, and having a sort of hood attached. The garment was fastened about the waist with a knotted rope. By this strange girdle the wearer was continually reminded that the body is a beast to be subdued by a halter.

[3] From the French frère.

On account of his learning, St. Anthony became a teacher of theology. He was connected successively with the universities of Bologna, Toulouse, Paris, and Padua, and with this last city his name has ever since been associated. At length, however, he forsook all other employments and devoted himself wholly to preaching among the people.

These were troublous times in Italy, when the poor were cruelly oppressed by the rich. St. Anthony espoused the cause of those who were wronged, and denounced all forms of tyranny. His influence was a great power among the people, and many stories are told of his preaching. It is related that one day, as he was explaining to his hearers the mystery of the Incarnation, the Christ-child appeared to him as in a vision.

It is this story which the painter had in mind in our picture: St. Anthony kneels before the mother and babe in an ecstasy of devotion. An open book lies on the ground beside him, as if he had been conning its pages when the vision broke upon him. The landscape surroundings are especially appropriate, for St. Anthony was fond of out-of-door life. His sermons were often given in the open air, and it is said that he sometimes preached to the fishes. He delighted to point out to his hearers the beauties of nature, the whiteness of the swan, the mutual charity of the storks, and the purity and fragrance of the lilies.

**THE VISION OF ST. ANTHONY**
**Brera Gallery, Milan**

The poetic refinement of his nature is indicated in his face. He is young and handsome, with the gentle expression which used to win the hearts of his hearers. There is little here to show the more forcible elements of his character. The tonsured head is the common mark of membership in religious orders.

The Christ-child bends forward to caress the saint's face with his tiny hand. He is a loving little fellow, not particularly pretty, except in his infantine plumpness, yet the face is full of innocent sweetness. A mysterious light shines above his head, the emblem of divinity. The good friar does not presume to touch the holy child, but folds his hands reverently across his breast. His eyes are lifted with the rapt look of the visionary.

St. Anthony's biographers tell us how he loved to recite the old Latin hymn by St. Fortunatus, beginning,—

O Gloriosa Domina
Excelsa super sydera.

[O most glorious Lady
Exalted above the stars.]

We may fancy that in the ecstasy of this vision these lines now rise to his lips. The last stanza expresses the sum of his adoration:—

Gloria tibi Domine
Qui natus es de Virgine
Cum Patre et sancto Spiritu
In sempiterna saecula.
[Glory to thee, O Lord,
Who wast born of a Virgin,
With the Father and Holy Spirit
For eternal ages.]

It is easy to see from a comparison of this picture with the Rest in Egypt that it was painted at about the same time. We at once recognize the mother and child of the other illustration, and note the similarity in pose. We may imagine the Madonna bending forward and holding the babe a little lower on her lap, and we should have the grouping as it is here.

In their pictures of the Madonna, the old painters tried to express their highest ideals of womanhood. The mother Mary represented to them all that is strongest and sweetest in a woman's character. So this Madonna by Van Dyck is a gracious and queenly figure modelled upon the stately Virgin of Titian.

The linear composition of the picture is carefully planned; the basis is the pyramidal form. From the top of the Virgin's head diverge the two oblique lines which enclose the diagram. The mantle fluttering behind the mother's shoulder balances the part of St. Anthony's tunic which lies on the ground.

We may well believe that the painter took especial pleasure in working on this picture, because he himself bore the name of the good St. Anthony.

# V

## MADAME ANDREAS COLYNS DE NOLE AND HER DAUGHTER

In the time of Van Dyck there was living in Antwerp a family of ancient lineage who bore the name of Colyns de Nole. For three centuries there had been sculptors among the men of this name. The talent had been handed down from father to son through the several generations, and sometimes there were two or three of the family working together in the art. The old churches of Antwerp contained some fine specimens of their work.[4]

[4] A full account of the several members of this family is given in the *Biographie Nationale*, published by the Royal Belgian Academy of Science, Literature and Fine Arts, Brussels, 1899.

Andreas Colyns de Nole was of nearly the same age as Van Dyck, and a worthy representative of his famous family. He was the sculptor of the beautiful monument of Henry van Balen in the Church of St. Jacques, and of a Pietà in the Church of Notre Dame. The sculptor and the painter became good friends, and it was a natural consequence that the latter should paint the portrait of his friend and of his family. He made two companion pictures, one of the sculptor, and the other of his wife and the little daughter.

The lady is seated in an arm-chair, letting her placid glance stray across the room. There is a little touch of weariness in her manner, as if she were glad to sit down for a few moments' rest. She is a busy housewife and mother, with many domestic duties on her mind. In her strong, capable way she has long borne the family burdens. The face is full of motherly sweetness; the expression is patient and serene, as of one well schooled in the lessons of life. This is indeed the "virtuous woman" whose price the wise man of old set "far above rubies."

"She openeth her mouth with wisdom; and in her tongue is the law of kindness. She looketh well to the ways of her household, and eateth not the bread of idleness. Her children arise up, and call her blessed; her husband also, and he praiseth her."[5]

[5] Proverbs, chapter xxx., verses 26-28.

The child is as like the mother as possible in features. Her round face is quaintly framed in a close lace-trimmed cap. She is a shy little creature, and is rather afraid of the strange painter. So she keeps as far as possible in the shelter of her mother's big sleeve. The hour drags wearily by. The studio is a dull place, and the sunshine without very inviting. The child pulls impatiently at her mother's arm, and, as the painter speaks, she looks timidly around, wondering what he will think of such a rude little girl.

**MADAME ANDREAS COLYNS DE NOLE AND HER DAUGHTER**
**Munich Gallery**

The artist is secretly much amused by the small young lady's behavior. He has a shrewd insight into children's thoughts, and sympathizes with their moods. He does not try to persuade her to sit for him, but he catches her pose just as she stands here. The mother, too, is wise enough to let the child alone, and the picture is made as we see it.

As we compare it with the former illustration of the man with his little boy, it is amusing to see the contrast between the two children. The boy has such a grave sense of responsibility, while the girl cares nothing for the portrait. She would doubtless think the boy very tiresome.

We are apt to think of the children of past centuries as altogether different beings from those of our own day. With few toys and books and pictures such as we have now, they must have been, we fancy, very sedate little creatures. A child portrait like this in our illustration dispels these false ideas. This little daughter of a seventeenth-century sculptor is as full of life and spirits as any child of to-day. Barring her quaint dress and foreign tongue she would be at home with children of her own age in any period or country.

The lady's dress is in a style similar to that which we have already studied in the portrait of our first illustration. The stiff bodice, with the long pointed front and square neck, the broad lace-trimmed collar, the large sleeves, and the wide cuffs turned back from the wrist, are details common to the two pictures. This costume, however, is somewhat less elegant than that of the English lady and more suggestive of every-day wear in the home. The collar is less elaborate, and not stiff; the neck is entirely covered with soft white material, fastened at the throat with a small brooch. A seal ring adorns each hand, worn on the index finger.

We recognize the pillar in the background as a common setting in Van Dyck's portraits. The taste of this time was rather artificial in such matters, and inclined to stateliness. There is here no vista beyond the pillar, no glimpse into another apartment, but the space is, as it were, completely walled in.

# VI

## DÆDALUS AND ICARUS

In the distant past which we call the age of fable lived the cunning craftsman Dædalus of Athens. One of his most curious inventions was a labyrinth which he constructed for Minos, the king of Crete. Having at length displeased this king he resolved to flee from the island with his son Icarus. It was impossible to escape by way of the sea without detection, but Dædalus was not discouraged.

"Land and wave,
He cried, deny me way! But Heaven above
Lies open! Heaven shall bear me home!"[6]

So saying he began to fashion some wings with which he might fly away. Feathers of different lengths were bound together with thread and wax, and shaped into arched pinions like those of a bird. As he worked, the boy Icarus stood by watching his father, and sometimes handling the feathers with his meddlesome fingers.

[6] All the quotations are from Ovid's *Metamorphoses*, Book viii., translated by Henry King.

At last the final touch was given, and Dædalus, fastening the wings to his body with wax, made a short trial flight. The invention was a success; the artist rose triumphant in the air. Then he taught his boy the use of the wings, warning him of every possible mishap:—

"'Midway keep thy course, he said,
My Icarus, I warn thee! if too low,
The damps will clog thy pinions; if too high,
The heats relax them. Midway hold thy flight.

By mine
Thy course direct.' And many a precept more
He gave, and careful as he bound the wings
Upon the shoulders of the boy, his cheeks
Were wet with tears, and in the task his hands
Paternal trembled."

Our picture illustrates this point in the story. Dædalus has just fastened the wings upon his son and is giving the final directions. The old man's face is full of anxiety, as he implores the lad not to fly too high. Icarus listens to the advice with a shade of impatience, pouting a little, like a wilful child who chafes under restraint. He points forward, as if to show that he understands his orders. Already the slender figure is poised for flight; he is eager to be off. In another moment he will rise into the air, dropping his garment as he ascends. A light breeze flutters the soft plumes of the wings and blows the loose curls about the boy's head. His youthful beauty, almost feminine in type, contrasts finely with the strong furrowed countenance of the father.

**DÆDALUS AND ICARUS**
**Collection of the Earl of Spencer, Althorp**

.

The story goes on to tell how the two started off together, the father leading the way.


"And, as the mother bird
When first her offspring from the nest essays
The air, he hovered anxious, cheering on

"The boy to follow, and with fatal art
Enjoining thus or thus his wings to ply
As he example gave."

For a while all went well, and they had covered a long distance, when Icarus,—

"Elate
With that new power, more daring grew, and left
His guide, and higher, with ambitious flight
Soared, aiming at the skies!"

This was the very danger against which Dædalus had warned his son.

"Upon his wings
The rays of noon struck scorching, and dissolved
The waxen compact of their plumes:—and down
He toppled, beating wild with naked arms
The unsustaining air, and with vain cry
Shrieking for succour from his sire!
The sea that bears his name received him as he fell."

Dædalus, having buried his son on the island of Icaria, proceeded on his way and came at last to Sicily, where he lived to finish some important works of architecture.

Our illustration shows some phases of Van Dyck's art with which we are least familiar. He rarely interested himself in mythological stories, though such subjects were common among his contemporaries. The painter has caught in this case the essential spirit of the myth. There are few of his pictures also in which he expressed so well the sense of motion. The inclination of the body of Icarus, the poise of the wings, and the gesture of the right hand all contribute admirably to this end.

Here, too, we see how carefully he studied the nude figure, and how well he understood the principles of modelling. The foreshortening of the right arm and hand of Icarus is a clever piece of technical workmanship. The composition is well planned to fill the canvas.

# VII

## PORTRAIT OF CHARLES I

*(By Sir Peter Lely, after Van Dyck)*

Charles I of England was the second king of the Stuart dynasty, whose despotic tendencies made the seventeenth century a memorable period in history. He ascended the throne at the age of twenty-five, and began at once to assert his belief in the divine right of kings. Indignant at the restraints which Parliament set upon his power, he dissolved this body and ruled alone.

For more than ten years he governed England in his own way, and during this time his court was conducted with great magnificence. The palace at Whitehall was the scene of many brilliant entertainments and lavish hospitalities.

Charles was an ardent lover of music, literature, and painting, and in his gallery was a collection of pictures remarkable for his time. He was particularly proud of the ceiling decorations of his Banqueting Hall, furnished by Rubens. He interested himself also in the manufacture of tapestries, and secured for England Raphael's cartoons for the Vatican tapestries, hoping thereby to raise the artistic standard of the home production.[7]

[7] See Chapter III. of volume on *Raphael* in the Riverside Art Series.

It was a crowning proof of his good taste that early in his reign he appointed Van Dyck the court painter. The Flemish painter was thereupon made Sir Anthony Van Dyck, and remained in the royal service until his death in 1641. It was the king's intention to have the walls of the Banqueting Hall decorated by Van Dyck, but this plan was never carried out. As it was, however, the court painter is said to have made, during his nine years' residence in England, no less than thirty-six portraits of the king, and twenty-five of the queen, Henrietta Maria, besides many pictures of their children, singly or in groups. His studio was a favorite resort of the royal pair, who used to come in their barge, by the way of the Thames, to his house at Blackfriars. The painter would receive them with the manners of a prince. Musicians played for their entertainment, and the conversation turned on questions of art.

In this constant intercourse, Van Dyck came to know well the face of his royal patron. It was not really a handsome face, as we see when we analyze the features in our illustration. The forehead is high but not broad, the nose large and not classically modelled, and the thick lips and weak curves of the mouth are not hidden by the upturned mustache. The shape of the face is long and narrow beyond good proportion, but this defect is relieved by the chestnut hair, which falls in long waving locks over the shoulders, and makes a broad frame for the face.

**PORTRAIT OF CHARLES I.**
**Dresden Gallery**

All these details, however, escape our attention when we look at the portrait for the first time. We are chiefly impressed by the kingly presence of the man. There is an indefinable suggestion of nobility in his bearing, an expression of grave dignity in his countenance. The eyes are almost melancholy, the glance is averted and remote. The consciousness of his royal birthright gives an air of aloofness to the figure.

The king stands beside a table, resting one hand on the broad rim of the hat which lies there, and holding his gloves in the other. He wears the mantle of the Order of the Garter, ornamented on the left side with the six-pointed silver star, in the centre of which is the red cross of St. George. From a broad blue ribbon about the neck is suspended a gold medallion. This is the "George," the image of the warrior saint, represented on horse-back in his encounter with the dragon.

The attempt of Charles to govern England without a Parliament proved a sad failure. He set his own authority above all laws, and persistently disregarded the rights of the people. At last he became involved in so many difficulties that he was obliged to reassemble the two houses. Then followed the long struggle between the king and the Parliament, which resulted in the Civil War. The supporters of the Crown represented chiefly the upper classes, and were called Cavaliers. The Parliamentarians were for the most part Puritans, and were men of fervent piety.

There were six years of fighting, beginning with the battle of Edgehill, and culminating in the Parliamentary victory at Naseby. Charles was tried and condemned as a "tyrant, traitor, murderer, and public enemy." On the 30th of January, 1649, he was executed in front of Whitehall Palace, walking to the scaffold with the same kingly dignity which he had shown throughout his life. "I go," said he, "from a corruptible to an incorruptible crown, where no disturbance can take place." His body was laid among others of England's royal dead at Windsor.

The picture reproduced in our illustration is not thought to be the original work of Van Dyck's hand, for that precious painting was destroyed by a fire in the Palace of Whitehall. It was a fortunate circumstance that while it was still in existence, Sir Peter Lely, court painter to Charles II., made a fine copy of it, which is now in the Dresden Gallery. A competent critic (Lionel Cust) tells us that the Dresden picture is so excellent that "it is difficult to believe it to be other than an original by Van Dyck."

AUTHORITIES.—Green: *A Short History of the English People;* D'Israeli: *Commentaries on the Life and Reign of Charles I.*

# VIII

## THE MADONNA OF ST. ROSALIA

On the summit of Monte Pellegrino, in the island of Sicily, stands a colossal statue of St. Rosalia. Like the old Greek statue of Victory on the island of Samothrace,[8] or to use a modern instance, like the statue of Liberty on Bedloe's Island in New York harbor, St. Rosalia serves as a beacon to mariners. The Sicilians hold the saint in great reverence, and celebrate her memory in two annual festivals. From the eleventh to the fifteenth of July are horse-races, regattas, illuminations, and all sorts of gayeties in her honor. In September there is a solemn procession to her chapel.

[8] See Chapter XV. in the volume on *Greek Sculpture* in the Riverside Art Series.

St. Rosalia was a Sicilian maiden of noble family, the niece of William II., called the Good. Being both rich and beautiful, she had many suitors for her hand, but she rejected them all. At the age of fifteen she renounced the pomps and vanities of the world, and devoted herself to a life of meditation. She retired secretly to a cavern on Mt. Heirkte, and here she passed her solitary life. It was not until five hundred years after her disappearance that her hiding-place was discovered. There they found her lying in her grotto, as if she had just fallen asleep, and on her head was a wreath of roses with which the angels had crowned her. The body was carried in triumph to Palermo, and she became the patron saint of her native city.

This was in the early part of the seventeenth century,[9] and the story of the new saint's life immediately became the subject of art. Van Dyck painted for a church in Antwerp a series of pictures of St. Rosalia, from which our illustration is taken. The maiden saint kneels on the steps of a throne to receive a wreath of roses from the Christ-child. An angel attendant behind her holds a basket of roses. St. Peter and St. Paul add dignity to the scene.

[9] The date of her disappearance is given as 1159.

As we see at once, this is not an actual incident from the life of St. Rosalia. The aim of the picture is devotional. It is as if we were given a glimpse into the court of heaven, where the saints of all ages gather about the Christ-child's throne.

St. Peter is seen at the Madonna's left, gazing at some little cherubs who hover in mid air with sprays of flowers. We know him by the mammoth key he carries in his left hand, a symbol of his authority in spiritual concerns. The reference is to the words of Jesus when Peter declared him to be the Christ: "I will give unto thee the keys of the kingdom of heaven."[10] He seems here a very old man, and one who has suffered many persecutions in the master's cause.

[10] St. Matthew, chapter xvi., verse 19.

**THE MADONNA OF ST. ROSALIA**
**Imperial Gallery, Vienna**

St. Paul stands at the right of the throne, leaning on his sword in an attitude of meditation. The sword has been chosen as this apostle's emblem because of his allusion in the Epistle to the Ephesians to the "sword of the spirit."[11] The books lying on the pavement at his feet are his various writings.

[11] Ephesians, chapter vi., verse 17.

According to tradition the Apostle Paul was a man of mean stature and insignificant appearance. Regardless of this fact, however, the old artists always tried to make him as grand and noble as possible, that his outward appearance might correspond to the grandeur of his character. There was a certain old Italian painter named Masaccio, who set the fashion, as it were, for the ideal portrait of St. Paul.[12] A hundred years later Raphael imitated this figure, and again a century later, Van Dyck repeated it in the picture before us. If we compare our illustration with a print of Raphael's picture of St. Cecilia we shall see the resemblance.[13] Even the pose is the same in the two cases. The grand head with the full beard reminds us of the Greeks' conception of their god Zeus.[14]

[12] In the fresco of the Carmine Church, Florence.

[13] See Chapter IX. of the volume on *Raphael* in the Riverside Art Series.

[14] See Chapter I. of the volume on *Greek Sculpture* in the Riverside Art Series.

St. Rosalia is a beautiful young woman, richly dressed in a brocaded mantle, and with wavy hair falling over her shoulders. Her attitude is very humble, and she lifts her face to the Christ-child's with sweet adoration. The little fellow seems delighted with his task, and leans forward eagerly, to offer the saint the crown of roses. Is it for me? she seems to ask, as she lays one hand upon her breast and timidly holds out the other.

On the step beside her is a human skull, across which lies a stalk of lilies. The flowers are an Easter emblem, and symbolize the Resurrection. The skull is the token of death. Thus are we taught the victory over death through the purity of the spiritual life.

The grotto of St. Rosalia has become a church which is the object of many a pious pilgrimage. It is for this that the name of the mountain was changed from Heirkte to Monte Pellegrino, which means the Pilgrim Mountain.

We have already seen (Chapters II. and IV.) how much Van Dyck owed to Titian in the rendering of sacred subjects. Here the Madonna's high throne beside the marble pillars, and the cherubs in mid air are striking reminiscences of Titian's Pesaro Madonna.[15]

[15] See Chapter XIV. in the volume on *Titian* in the Riverside Art Series.

# IX

## CHARLES, PRINCE OF WALES

*(Detail of Children of Charles I.)*

The Prince Charles of our picture was the son of Charles I. and Henrietta Maria, and bore the title of the Prince of Wales. He was born on the morning of May 29, 1630, and there was great rejoicing in the royal household that he was a fine strong baby. The king at once rode in state to St. Paul's Cathedral to give thanks for the birth of an heir. While the procession was on its way a bright star appeared in the noonday sky. This was hailed as a good omen, and an epigram was composed on the occasion:—

"When to Paul's Cross the grateful King drew near,
A shining star did in the heavens appear.
Thou that consultest with bright mysteries
Tell me what this bright wanderer signifies?"
"Now there is born a valiant prince i' the west,
That shall eclipse the kingdoms of the east."

A month later the baby's baptism was celebrated with great solemnity in the chapel at St. James. The famous Laud, Bishop of London, officiated, and the sponsors were Louis XIII. of France, Marie de Médicis, and the Elector Palatine, all represented by proxies. There were wonderful christening presents, among them a jewel of great value brought by the old Duchess of Richmond.

The new-born prince did not grow into a pretty baby. Even his mother, who would naturally wish to praise him, wrote to a friend in France that he was "so ugly she was ashamed of him." "But," she added, "his size and fatness supply the want of beauty. I wish you could see the gentleman, for he has no ordinary mien; he is so serious in all that he does that I cannot help deeming him far wiser than myself." A few years later the child became a pretty boy, with a fine figure, brown complexion, and large, bright black eyes. His mouth, however, remained very ugly.

The prince's earliest years were passed happily, and no one could have foreseen the stormy experiences through which he must pass before he should inherit the throne of his father. The king and queen were devoted to each other and to their children. There was a younger boy, Prince James, and three sisters, to complete the family circle.[16] It is pleasant to imagine them at play in the royal nursery.

[16] That is, Princess Mary, Princess Elizabeth, and Princess Anne. Prince Henry was only an infant when the family circle was broken up, and Princess

Henrietta was not born until 1644, while the Civil War was actually in progress.

The young Prince of Wales had for his governor the Earl of Newcastle. We read of a letter written at the age of eight and addressed to this nobleman.

**CHARLES, PRINCE OF WALES**
**Royal Gallery, Turin**

The contents refer wittily to the governor's advice about taking medicine:—

"My lord,

"I would not have you take too much phisike for it doth always make me worse; and I think it will doe the like with you. I ride every day, and am ready to follow any other directions from you. Make haste back to him that loves you,

"Charles P."

We see from this that the boy was early taught to ride, and was doubtless trained in all manly sports. In the Stuart household dogs were the favorite pets, and the young Charles seems always to have been accompanied by one, now a collie, now a spaniel, now a great boarhound. The queen had a peculiar fancy for dwarfs, which were in this period common playthings of royalty. Little Geoffrey Hudson, eighteen inches high, was an important member of the court, having been presented to Henrietta Maria in a huge pie.[17]

[17] As we read in Scott's novel, Peveril of the Peak.

In our picture Prince Charles is about five years old. At this age, in our modern fashions, a boy is dressed quite differently from a girl. Here, however, the little prince's finery and his round lace cap somewhat belie his manliness. Yet his short hair cut in a straight fringe across the forehead is his boy's prerogative. The wide lace collar was worn by men as well as boys, as we may see in the portraits of the king and of the Duke of Lennox. We speak of it to-day as a "Van Dyck collar."

The child has a winning face, with large round eyes and a mouth which the flattering painter has shaped like a Cupid's bow. Though the expression is perfectly child-like, there is a certain dignity in the pose of the head, which makes the boy appear mature beyond his years. Evidently Van Dyck meant everybody to know that this was a prince.

Prince Charles's happy boyhood came to an end at the breaking out of the Civil War. Though he was then only twelve years of age, he and his brother, Prince James, followed their father to the battlefield, suffering cold and hunger and even the dangers of the enemy's bullets. At the age of sixteen, the Prince of Wales joined his mother in Paris. Upon the execution of his father he at once assumed the title of King Charles II., and in the following year was crowned at Scone in Scotland at the age of twenty-one. Putting himself at the head of the Scottish army, he advanced into England, and was completely defeated by Cromwell. After nine years of exile he was recalled to England and restored to the throne. Thus did the innocent baby prince of our picture become the Merry Monarch of the Restoration, whose court was a disgrace in English history.

Our illustration is a detail of a larger picture containing a group of three children, Prince Charles, with Princess Mary and Prince James, Duke of York.

AUTHORITY.—Strickland: *Queens of England.*

# X

## ST. MARTIN DIVIDING HIS CLOAK WITH A BEGGAR

St. Martin was born during the reign of the Emperor Constantine the Great, and was the son of a Roman soldier. He himself entered the army at an early age, and was sent into Gaul with a regiment of cavalry. Among his comrades he was loved for his mildness of temper and his generosity.

It happened that he was stationed in the city of Amiens, during a winter of unusual severity. There was great suffering among the poor, and many perished with cold and hunger. St. Martin was riding one day through the city gate, when he passed a naked beggar shivering on the pavement. Immediately he drew rein, and spoke pityingly to the poor creature. The young soldier was wearing over his coat of mail a long mantle. Slipping this garment from his shoulders he divided it with his sword, giving half to the beggar. That same night, as he slept, he had a vision of Jesus clad in the portion of his mantle. And Jesus, turning to the angels who accompanied him, said, "My servant Martin hath done this."

After a time St. Martin left the army, to devote himself wholly to a religious life. He became the Bishop of Tours, and was noted for his deeds of mercy and charity. It was always his delight to clothe the poor. Once while he was standing at the altar of the cathedral, he turned and threw his priestly garment over a beggar, with the same impulsive generosity which had led him to divide his military cloak. He was zealous also in uprooting all forms of heathenism, and cast down many temples of idols.

He lived to a good old age, and died among the scenes of his labors. The legend relates that as he lay in his last illness he prayed his brethren to move him where he might see more of heaven than of earth. His face shone as it had been glorified, and the voices of angels were heard singing.[18] In Tours from that day to this his memory is piously cherished. Every child in the street loves to tell the story of the gallant soldier who shared his cloak with the beggar.

[18] The life of St. Martin is related with much circumstance in the *Golden Legend*. See Caxton's translation in the *Temple Classics Edition*, vol. vi., p. 142. Mrs. Jameson gives a brief account of the same in *Sacred and Legendary Art*, p. 705.

This is the story in our picture. St. Martin rides forward on a splendid white charger, accompanied by other horsemen. At the corner of the gateway two beggars await them. The older one hobbles forward on his knees, supported by crutches. Though he is a miserable object, he is fairly protected from the cold by a long garment. His companion is perfectly naked, a huge muscular fellow seated on some straw. He is just turning about to make way for the cavalcade, when the knight draws rein.

**ST. MARTIN DIVIDING HIS CLOAK WITH A BEGGAR**
**Church of Saventhem**

The horse arches his neck proudly and stamps impatient at the delay. The rider on St. Martin's right looks across with surprise. But the young knight serenely proceeds in his generous act. Already his cloak has slipped from his figure and hangs only from his left shoulder. Grasping it with his left hand half way down its length, he raises his sword to sunder it at this place.

The lower end has fallen across the beggar's right arm. At its warm touch, the man, overwhelmed with gratitude, abashed perhaps by the goodness of his benefactor, hides his face with his upraised left arm. It is as if the knightly purity of the compassionate face above him has revealed the man to himself in his loathsome degradation.

The young soldier is clad in a tunic of mail which sets off to perfect advantage the lithe figure. Over his short curls is worn a jaunty cap with a long feather; he is a veritable fairy prince. The boyish face accords well with the legend, which relates that he was only a youth when the incident occurred. It is said that no one ever saw St. Martin angry, or sad, or gay; he was always sweet, and serious, and serene. This, too, is precisely as we see him in the picture. The good deed done, we may fancy the young cavalier riding on his way, as if nothing had happened.

The beautiful horse of the picture is one which appears in many of Van Dyck's works. There is a tradition that the original was Rubens's gift to the painter when he set out for Italy. Van Dyck has built his picture on a diagonal plan, such as the older painter Rubens often used. The main line of the composition runs from the head of the man in the upper left corner, to the beggar in the lower right corner. The lifted sword and the falling mantle form the connecting lines across the canvas.

The feast of St. Martin is celebrated on the eleventh of November, in that short season of warm weather which brightens the autumn. It is for this that the French call the week "St. Martin's little summer." Every year, at this time, pious pilgrims visit the quiet cells, in the limestone cliff by the riverside, where the good bishop used to retire for prayer.

# XI

## THE CRUCIFIXION

The life of our Lord, which began in the Bethlehem manger, culminated on the cross of Mount Calvary. In our picture we see the Man of Sorrows in his last moments of suffering. How it came about that he was crucified is fully related by the four evangelists.[19]

[19] St. Matthew, chapters xxvi. and xxvii.; St. Mark, chapters xiv. and xv.; St. Luke, chapters xxii. and xxiii.; St. John, chapters xviii. and xix.

For three years he had gone about among the people, healing the sick, comforting the sorrowing, and preaching the good tidings of the kingdom. His blameless life was a constant reproach to hypocrites and evil doers. The priests were jealous of his popularity and hated him for his rebukes. As the feast of the Passover drew near, they sought how they might kill him.

Judæa was at that time a province of the great Roman empire, and the civil authority was vested in the governor, Pontius Pilate, and a body of Roman soldiery. The Romans, however, did not interfere much with the affairs of the Jews, and there was little trouble in carrying out a plot. A formal charge against Jesus was made by false witnesses, and he was arrested as a common criminal. After being examined by the high priest, he was led to the governor for trial. "And they began to accuse him, saying, We found this fellow perverting the nation and forbidding to give tribute to Cæsar, saying that he himself is Christ, a king."

Pilate now took him within his palace for a private interview, and could find no fault with him. Nor did King Herod, to whom the case was referred, differ from the governor as to the prisoner's innocence. Pilate therefore appealed to the people in behalf of Jesus, but a multitude of angry voices shouted, "Crucify him!" "Crucify him!" "And so, Pilate, willing to content the people ... delivered Jesus ... to be crucified." He was crucified, as we know, between two thieves, and over his cross was the superscription written by Pilate, in three languages, "This is Jesus, the King of the Jews."

Seven times, while he hung upon the cross, did the suffering Saviour speak aloud. "Father, forgive them," was his first exclamation, "for they know not what they do." His next words were to the thief on one side, who begged to be remembered when Jesus should come into His own: "This day shalt thou be with me in Paradise," was the reply. Then his thoughts turned lovingly to his mother, who stood with John by the cross. "Woman, behold thy son," he said to her, indicating John. Then turning to John, he added, "Behold thy mother." A moment of agony followed, when he cried, "My God, my God, why hast thou forsaken me?" After this, he said, "I thirst," and a soldier held to his lips a sponge wet with vinegar. As the end drew near came the words, "It is finished," and at last, "Father, into thy hands I commend my spirit."

**THE CRUCIFIXION**
**Antwerp Museum**

In Van Dyck's picture we see nothing of the surroundings of the Crucifixion—the Roman soldiers, the curious crowd, the sorrowing friends, or the crucified thieves. Only the solitary figure of Jesus, nailed to the cross, is lifted against the strange dark sky. For three hours, as we read, there was darkness over all the land, followed immediately, after the death of Jesus, by a great earthquake. This is the moment when the storm-clouds are gathering over the face of the sun, causing its light to gleam luridly through the thick covering. The cross is rudely built of two beams in the form which is called a Latin cross. A fluttering scroll at the top of the upright beam carries the accusation "The King of the Jews."

The garments of Jesus had been stripped from his body and divided among four soldiers. He now hangs naked upon the cross save a small strip of cloth knotted about his loins, the loose ends hanging at one side. The body is somewhat slender and delicately modelled, but firm and supple as of one in the fulness of manhood. The hair falls in dishevelled locks about the face, and a mysterious light shines above the head.

As we look at the picture, each one must decide for himself what moment in the great drama is illustrated. From the expression of suffering on the countenance we judge that the end is approaching. From the lifted face and open mouth we see that the sufferer communes with his Father.

The Crucifixion is the saddest subject a painter could choose, yet notwithstanding this, it has been one of the most important subjects in Christian art. Van Dyck painted it many times, and expressed, as we see here, a deep sense of the tragic nature of the scene. Yet he always avoided those harrowing details which make some of the pictures of the older masters too painful to contemplate. For this reason his crucified Christ has been chosen as the model for the Crucifixion scene in the Passion Play at Ober-Ammergau.

We may see how wide was the range of our artist's gifts, which extended from such joyous pictures as the Rest in Egypt to a theme so solemn as the Crucifixion.

# XII

## JAMES STUART, DUKE OF LENNOX AND AFTERWARDS OF RICHMOND

James Stuart, Duke of Lennox, was one of the most prominent personages at the English court. His uncle was a cousin and trusted friend of King James I., and the relations between the nephew and Charles I. were even closer. Immediately upon taking a degree at Cambridge, the young nobleman entered the royal service as Gentleman of the King's Bedchamber. He was just thirteen years of age, and a born courtier. "His courtesie was his nature, not his craft," quaintly says one historian. While still in his minority, he visited France, Italy, and Spain. When Van Dyck came to England, he became at once one of the painter's most frequent sitters.

Our illustration is one of the first of the series of portraits of the Duke of Lennox, and shows him at the age of twenty. The young man stands with his hand on the head of a favorite greyhound, and turns his pleasant face to ours with a smile. He wears the habit of the Order of the Garter. This "most noble and illustrious Order" was instituted by King Edward III. under the patronage of St. George. It consisted of the sovereign and twenty-five "companions" banded together, like the knights of Arthur's Round Table, for the advancement of ideal manliness. The ceremony of investiture was very solemn, each part of the costume being placed in turn on the elect knight, when he knelt to take the vows. We note in the picture the same details which we saw in the portrait of Charles I., the mantle with the great silver star, and the gold medal, or "George," on the blue ribbon. One part of the costume not to be seen in the other picture is the garter, worn on the left leg "between the knee and the calf," as the old directions read.

The garter was, indeed, originally the most important emblem of the entire garb. It symbolized to the wearers that "as by their Order, they were join'd in a firm League of Amity and Concord, so by their Garter, as by a fast Tye of Affection, they were obliged to love one another." The garter was blue, fastened with a gold buckle, and on it was inscribed the motto, "Honi soit qui mal y pense" [Evil to him who evil thinks]. A miniature representation of the garter encircles the cross in the centre of the star, and also forms a border of the "George" medallion.

From the broad lace collar to the high-heeled shoes with their huge rosettes, the young man of the picture represents the height of the prevailing fashion. His hair is carefully curled in the manner of the Cavaliers. He is in fact the impersonation of the court life of the period. It is pleasant to fancy the graceful youth moving through the stately figures of the court dances.

**JAMES STUART, DUKE OF LENNOX AND RICHMOND**
Metropolitan Art Museum, New York

It was five years after this portrait was painted that the Duke of Lennox married Mary, the daughter of the first Duke of Buckingham. Then followed the troubles in Scotland caused by the king's persistent attempt to force the liturgy of the Church of England upon the people. Lennox now showed himself a stanch adherent of the Crown, and upheld the royal cause in the face of the bitter opposition of the Scotch. His enemies thought him very haughty and severe in his manner, but his probity and sincerity seem not to have been questioned.

In 1641, he was created Duke of Richmond, and in the same year was appointed to the high office of Lord Steward of the Household. Throughout the civil war he served his royal master with untiring faithfulness, devoting a large part of his fortune to the cause of the Crown. When Charles was held a prisoner in Hampton Court, it was this friend who cheered the period of his confinement. When at last, after the execution of the king, the royal remains were buried at Windsor, the Duke of Richmond was one of the four noblemen who sorrowfully bore the pall to the grave. He died in the prime of manhood, in 1655.

A more loyal follower no king could have, yet, notwithstanding his zeal, the Duke of Lennox and Richmond failed to exert any great influence upon history, because he lacked the necessary judgment and decision of character. His portrait certainly does not indicate any special intellectual promise in the young man. Yet the face is so refined, the expression so winning, that none can help feeling the singular charm of the personality. Van Dyck understood well how to impart an air of distinction to a figure, and when, as in this case, he had a favorable subject, he was especially successful.

To lovers of dogs the greyhound is no unimportant part of our picture. The painter has expressed with much insight the character of this beautiful and high-bred creature. The muzzle is pressed affectionately to the master's side, and the eyes are fixed upon the beloved face with an expression of intense devotion. There is a tradition that this animal once saved the duke's life by rousing him from sleep at the approach of an assassin.

In the making up of the composition, the dog's figure describes a diagonal line on the left, which balances a similar diagonal on the other side made by the duke's placing his arm akimbo. Thus the general diagram of a pyramid is suggested as the basis of the grouping.

AUTHORITIES.—Robert Vaughn: *The History of England under the House of Stuarts*; L. von Ranke: *The History of England in the Seventeenth Century*; Warwick's *Memoirs*; Doyle's *Official Baronage of England*.

# XIII

## CHRIST AND THE PARALYTIC

It was a part of our Lord's ministry among men to restore to health the body as well as the soul. He was often moved with compassion by the disease and suffering which he saw as he went about Galilee or passed through the streets of Jerusalem. St. John, the evangelist (chapter v.), relates an incident which took place at a pool called Bethesda near a sheep market in Jerusalem.

There were here five porches in which lay "a great multitude of impotent folk, of blind, halt, withered, waiting for the moving of the water." It seems that at certain intervals the waters of the pool were troubled, as if moved by some unseen agency. It was believed that the first person stepping in thereafter would be healed of any disease he might have.

"And a certain man was there, which had an infirmity thirty and eight years. When Jesus saw him lie, and knew that he had been now a long time in that case, he saith unto him, Wilt thou be made whole? The impotent man answered him, Sir, I have no man, when the water is troubled, to put me into the pool: but while I am coming, another steppeth down before me. Jesus saith unto him, Rise, take up thy bed, and walk. And immediately the man was made whole, and took up his bed, and walked."[20]

[20] There was another case of Christ's healing a paralytic, but as on that occasion the sick man's bed was let down through the roof into a house, the incident does not fit the picture so well as that of Bethesda.

This is the incident illustrated by our picture. Jesus has already brought the paralytic to his feet, and now sends him on his way. Two other men complete the group, but take no part in the conversation. One is a disciple, perhaps John, who accompanies the Master, the other is a spectator peering curiously over the paralytic's shoulder.

The restored paralytic carries under one arm a rug, which has been clumsily rolled into a bundle. This is the sort of "bed" used among the poor of Eastern countries. He is but half clad in a garment which slips from his shoulders, showing his emaciated form. The face is sharpened by suffering; he is altogether a strange and repulsive figure. Like the beggar who lay in St. Martin's path he represents a degraded class of humanity.

He leans now towards his unknown friend in a pitiable effort to express his gratitude. The eyes have a look of dumb devotion like those of a faithful dog. He lays one hand humbly upon his breast. Jesus turns to the poor creature with an expression of infinite compassion. He reads the man's heart with his searching glance. Thanks he does not need; his first care is to send the man forth to begin life anew.

**CHRIST AND THE PARALYTIC**
**Buckingham Palace**

The head of the Saviour is painted after the ideal portrait which has been handed down from generation to generation since the early days of Christianity. The oval face with classical features, the full beard, the long hair parted in the middle, such are the familiar features which we have all come to associate with the person of Jesus. Yet notwithstanding this general similarity in the many pictures of Christ, every great artist has brought out something different in the face.

It was Titian's peculiar glory to show the intellectual side of our Lord's character as no other Italian had done. Van Dyck, with characteristic admiration for the great Venetian, followed his example. If we compare our illustration with Titian's Christ of the Tribute Money[21] we shall see how closely the former imitates the latter. Yet, as no man of imagination can copy exactly another's work, Van Dyck's ideal of Christ is less ascetic than Titian's and somewhat more benign. In both pictures the pure countenance of the Saviour is sharply contrasted with the coarse face beside him.

[21] See Chapter VIII. of the volume on *Titian* in the Riverside Art Series.

We are interested to read on in St. John's narrative the sequel of the story illustrated in our picture. It happened to be the Sabbath day, and, as the restored paralytic passed through the city, the Jews said unto him: "It is not lawful for thee to carry thy bed."

"He answered them, He that made me whole, the same said unto me, Take up thy bed, and walk. Then asked they him, What man is that which said unto thee, Take up thy bed, and walk? And he that was healed wist not who it was: for Jesus had conveyed himself away, a multitude being in that place.

"Afterward Jesus findeth him in the temple and said unto him, Behold, thou art made whole: sin no more, lest a worse thing come unto thee. The man departed, and told the Jews that it was Jesus, which had made him whole."

# XIV

## PHILIP, LORD WHARTON

Philip, Lord Wharton, was an English nobleman of nearly the same age as the Duke of Lennox, and the two were painted by Van Dyck at about the same time. In both young men are apparent the same signs of gentle birth and breeding, a dignity of bearing, and a repose of manner characteristic of their class. That they were quite different in essential character, however, we shall presently see.

Lord Wharton was the fourth baron of his family and the second of the name Philip. He succeeded to his title as he was entering his teens, and at the age of nineteen he had become one of the most attractive figures at the court of Charles I. In this year he married Elizabeth, the daughter of Sir Rowland Wandesford. It was in honor of this occasion that the portrait of our illustration was painted.

Of a lover so handsome and graceful, the promised bride may well have been proud. His dress is rich and picturesque: the jacket is of violet velvet, the mantle of yellow satin, and the costume is set off by delicate laces at the throat and wrists. These were days when the men vied with women in fondness for finery.

Lord Wharton was at this time on terms of friendly intimacy with the king and queen. It was a flattering mark of royal favor when the king presented the young courtier with two full-length portraits of himself and of Queen Henrietta, painted by Van Dyck. Perhaps the artistic tastes they had in common formed the bond of friendship between them. Lord Wharton, it appears, admired Van Dyck's portrait work almost as much as King Charles. On his second marriage, five years later, he employed the artist to paint a number of family portraits. He prized these so highly that he built a gallery specially for them in his new house at Winchendon.

The time soon came when more strenuous questions occupied him. The contest between the king and the Parliament brought every Englishman to a parting of the ways. Lord Wharton was a Puritan, and took a decided stand on the side of Parliament. His personal relations with the king were outweighed by his sense of patriotic duty.

At the breaking out of the war he entered the Parliamentary army, serving successively as colonel of a regiment of foot, and as a captain of a troop of horse. He took part in the battle of Edgehill, and was brought into considerable prominence at this time. In a famous speech made soon afterwards, he charged the king's nephew, Prince Rupert, with gross "inhumanity and barbarousness" during the course of the battle. Evidently where his mind was made up, Lord Wharton was a strong partisan.

**PHILIP, LORD WHARTON**
**Hermitage Gallery, St. Petersburg**

Of this we should suspect nothing from our portrait. It is hard to imagine that this beardless young courtier, so suave and amiable in appearance, will ten years later be fighting sternly against his king. Here his thoughts seem to be wholly romantic: his eyes have the dreamy expression of an expectant lover. His is surely a knightly soul unstained by worldliness. The face is of that perfect oval admired by artists as the highest standard of beauty. Taste and refinement are the most striking qualities one reads in it; the mouth is the most individual feature, small and modelled in delicate curves. Yet with all its sweetness, those firmly closed lips suggest tenacity of opinion and strength of will.

As the event proved, Lord Wharton was a man of uncompromising political opinions. He was at one time committed to the Tower on a charge of contempt of the House. In his long and active life he saw England pass through many changes. He was an old man when the last of the Stuart kings

(James II.) fled from England, leaving a vacant throne. Macaulay tells us of the Whig nobleman's speech in the meeting of the Lords which resulted in the invitation to William and Mary of Orange to take the government. He knew how to be fair as well as severe, and a still later speech is recorded when he opposed the Abjuration Bill.[22] He died at the age of eighty-five in 1698.

[22] This bill provided that no person should sit in either house of Parliament or hold any office without making declaration that he would stand by William and Mary against James and his adherents.

There are other portraits by Van Dyck more vigorous than this, but none perhaps more charming. As we have seen in the portrait of the Duke of Lennox, the painter was nowhere more successful than in portraying the young courtier. We recognize the pose, with one arm akimbo, as a favorite device of Van Dyck. While in some cases it seems artificial, here it appears to be an attitude which the young man assumed of his own accord.

On his left arm he carries a tall shepherd's staff; it may be that he has sometime played a pastoral part in some masque. His costume, however, does not accord with such a part, and it is more likely that the staff is held merely to give some use to the left hand. We note in another illustration that the man called Richardot holds a book, with his hand in a similar position.

The texture painting of Lord Wharton's costume is skilfully rendered, and a rich satin hanging behind him throws a part of the figure into relief. On the other side is a glimpse of landscape lighting the composition pleasantly with a distant view.

Authorities.—Macaulay: *History of England*; Doyle's *Official Baronage of England*.

# XV

## THE LAMENTATION OVER CHRIST

A great company of people had followed Jesus to his crucifixion, including not only his enemies, but his friends. The beloved disciple John was accompanied by Mary. "And many women were beholding afar off, which followed Jesus from Galilee, ministering unto him; among which was Mary Magdalene, and Mary the mother of James and Joses, and the mother of Zebedee's children.

"When the even was come there came a rich man of Arimathea named Joseph, who also himself was Jesus' disciple. He went to Pilate and begged the body of Jesus. Then Pilate commanded the body to be delivered. And when Joseph had taken the body, he wrapped it in a clean linen cloth, and laid it in his own new tomb which he had hewn out in the rock: and he rolled a great stone to the door of the sepulchre and departed."[23]

[23] St. Matthew, chapter XXVII., verses 55-60.

During all this time two at least of the original company of women had lingered near while the body of Jesus was taken from the cross and made ready for burial. They were the mother Mary and Mary Magdalene. Even after Joseph's task was done and he had gone his way, they remained "sitting over against the sepulchre."

It is not unnatural to suppose that they may have had some share in the preparation of the body. Nicodemus, as we learn elsewhere, had brought a mixture of myrrh and aloes, which it was the custom of the Jews to use in burial.[24] Both men must have been glad of the presence and help of the faithful women.

[24] St. John, chapter XIX., verse 39.

Poets and painters have dwelt much on these sad moments, supplying from the imagination the details omitted in the narrative. The women must at times have been unable to restrain their tears; natural grief must have its way. Then might the men have left them awhile alone with their dead, as they busied themselves with their task.

It is some such idea as this which inspired the painting of our illustration. The mother Mary supports the head of her son upon her bosom; Mary Magdalene stoops to kiss the lifeless hand; St. John approaches at one side with a mantle.

The body of Christ, wrapped in a cloth, has been laid upon a rock in a cavern. The agony of his cruel death is past, and the face is calm as of one who sleeps. The figure is, as we have seen it on the cross, robust and well knit. Only the nail prints in hands and feet show the manner of his dying. On the ground beside him is a basin with a sponge, surrounded by tokens of the crucifixion, the crown of thorns, the nails, and the superscription.

**THE LAMENTATION OVER CHRIST**
**Antwerp Museum**

We see in the Madonna the same stately and beautiful woman who carried her babe on the journey to Egypt. Her veil is now drawn well over her head, entirely concealing her hair. She has borne the cares of life with courage, and the years have touched her face but lightly. Even in the hour of anguish she lifts her eyes to heaven with resignation, yet one hand is extended with a gesture which seems to implore mercy.

Mary Magdalene is a much younger woman. She has peculiar reason for her devotion to Jesus, for he saved her from a strange fate.[25] Her impulsive and loving nature is now overwhelmed with grief. Her rich costume is in disorder, and her hair falls in loose locks over her shoulders. Her lovely face is very sad. Half kneeling, she presses her lips to the wound in the left hand. Her attitude and manner are full of humility, as if she felt herself unworthy to approach too near.

[25] St. Luke, chapter VIII., verse 2.

St. John regards the group with gentle sympathy. He is spoken of as "the disciple whom Jesus loved," so intimate was the relation between them. To his care Jesus intrusted the Mother Mary, and he now remains near as one of the few most deeply bereaved. He is very young, with a sensitive face and delicately cut features.

The subject of the picture is one which Van Dyck treated in several compositions. The Flemish title is "Nood Godes," the suffering of God. The Italians call it the Pietà, which means, compassion. One of the most celebrated works of art devoted to the theme is the marble group in Rome by Michelangelo.[26] Van Dyck must have seen this work on his visit to the Eternal City, and was no doubt inspired in some measure by its grandeur. We notice that in his picture the Mother extends her left hand in a gesture similar to that of the marble figure.

[26] See Chapter VI. in the volume on *Michelangelo* in the Riverside Art Series.

# XVI

## PORTRAIT OF VAN DYCK

The painter Van Dyck was the son of a rich merchant of Antwerp, and lacked no opportunities for the training of his artistic gifts. He was fortunate also in meeting ready appreciation wherever he went. In Italy, in Flanders, and finally in England, his paintings were highly valued. His life was passed amid luxurious surroundings, in the society of noblemen and princes. His was a brilliant and successful career.

Our portrait frontispiece was painted during his residence in England, when he was about forty years of age. He is described as short in stature, with a slender figure. His hands were long, with the straight sensitive fingers of the artist. He had a fresh delicate face, with well-cut features, and light chestnut-colored hair, which he wore long, like the English Cavaliers. The upturned mustache and small pointed beard were also fashionable among the English nobility, as we infer from the portrait of Charles I.

The face has the characteristic qualities of the artistic nature, the high forehead, the dreamy eyes, and the pensive expression. The head is lifted a little, in an imaginative pose. We should know this man at once for a poet or a painter.

It must be confessed that we do not find much strength of character in the face. Van Dyck indeed lacked the nobler qualities of manliness, and was decidedly worldly in his tastes. He lived in princely magnificence in his house at Blackfriars, spending money lavishly. A biographer tells how "he always went magnificently Drest, had a numerous and gallant Equipage, and kept so noble a Table in his Apartment that few Princes were more visited or better serv'd."

To maintain this expensive establishment the painter was obliged to devote his mornings to hard work in his studio. The nights were spent in banquets and revelry. Naturally his health gave way under the strain of this double life. While he still cherished ambitious projects for greater works of art, he sickened and died in London at the age of forty-two.

Two years before this he had married an English lady, Mary Ruthven, and they had one child, a daughter.

Our frontispiece is a detail of a double portrait representing, in half-length figures, the painter and a patron, John Digby, Earl of Bristol.

The Diacritical Marks given are those found in the latest edition of Webster's International Dictionary.

EXPLANATION OF DIACRITICAL MARKS.

A Dash (¯) above the vowel denotes the long sound, as in fāte, ēve, tīme, nōte, ūse.

A Dash and a Dot (-) above the vowel denote the same sound, less prolonged.

A Curve (˘) above the vowel denotes the short sound, as in ădd, ĕnd, ĭll, ŏdd, ŭp.

A Dot ( ) above the vowel a denotes the obscure sound of a in påst, åbāte, Amĕricå.

A Double Dot (¨) above the vowel a denotes the broad sound of a in fäther, älms.

A Double Dot (..) below the vowel a denotes the sound of a in ba̤ll.

A Wave (~) above the vowel e denotes the sound of e in hẽr.

A Circumflex Accent (^) above the vowel o denotes the sound of o in bôrn.

A dot (.) below the vowel u denotes the sound of u in the French language.

N indicates that the preceding vowel has the French nasal tone.

G and K denote the guttural sound of ch in the German language.

th denotes the sound of th in the, this.

ç sounds like s.

c͡ sounds like k.

ṣ sounds like z.

ḡ is hard as in ḡet.

ġ is soft as in ġem.

- Amiens (ä-mĕ-ăN').
- Andreas (än-drā'äs).
- Anne (ăn).
- Anthony (ăn'tō-nĭ).

- Antwerp (ănt'wērp).
- Arimathea (Ărĭmȧthē´ȧ).
- Assisi (ä-sē'sē).
- Astolat (ăs'tó̄-lăt).
- Athens (ăth'ĕnz).
- Bedloe (bĕd'lō).
- Belgium (bĕl'jĭ-ŭm).
- Bentivoglio (bĕn-tē-vōl'yō).
- Bethesda (bĕ-thĕz'dȧ).
- Bethlehem (Bĕth'lēhĕm).
- Biographie Nationale (bé̄-ó̄-grä-fē' nä-sé̄-ó̄-näl').
- Blackfriars (blăk'frī-ẽrz).
- Bologna (bō-lōn'yȧ).
- Bristol (brĭs'tol̪).
- Brussels (brŭs'ĕlz).
- Buckingham (bŭk'ĭng-ȧm).
- Cæsar (sē'zȧr).
- Calvary (kăl'vȧ-rĭ).
- Carmine (kär'mē-nā).
- Cavaliers (kăv-ȧ-lērz').
- Caxton (kăks'tŭn).
- Cecilia (sē-sĭl-ĭ-ȧ).
- Colyns de Nole (kó̄-lăN dē̃ nōl).
- Constantine (kŏn'stȧn-tīn).
- Cromwell (Crŏm'wĕll).
- Crowe (krō).
- Cupid (Cū'pĭd).
- Cust, Lionel (kŭst lī'ō-nĕl).

- Dædalus (dĕd'ȧ-lŭs or dē'dȧ-lŭs).
- Digby (dĭg'bĭ).
- D'Israeli (dĭz-rā'lĭ).
- Doyle (doil).
- Dresden (drĕz'de̱n).
- Edgehill (ĕj'hĭl).
- Egypt (ē'jĭpt).
- Elizabeth (ḗ-lĭz'ȧ-bĕth).
- Ephesians (ē-fē'zhȧnz).
- Eugenia (ū-jē'nĭ-ȧ).
- Flanders (flăn'dẽrz).
- Florence (Flôr'ĕnce).
- Fortunatus (Fôrtūnā'tŭs).
- Franciscan (frăn sĭs'kȧn).
- *frère* (frăr).
- Fromentin (frṓ-mŏN-tăN').
- Galilee (găl'ĭ-lē).
- Genoa (jĕn'ō-ȧ).
- Hampton (hămp'to̱n).
- Heirkte (hīrk'tē).
- Henrietta Maria (Hĕnrĭĕt'tȧ Mȧrī'ȧ).
- Herod (Hĕr'o̱d).
- Honi soit qui mal y pense (ŏn-ē' swä kē mäl ē päNs).
- Hudson, Geoffrey (hŭd'so̱n jĕf'frī ).
- Icaria (ī-kā'rĭ-ȧ).
- Icarus (ĭk'ȧ-rŭs).
- Italy (ĭt'ȧ-lĭ).
- Jacques (zhäk).

- Jameson (jā'mĕ-sŭn).
- Jerusalem (Jĕrū'sȧlĕm).
- Joses (jō'sēz).
- Judæa (jū dē'ȧ).
- Knackfuss (knäk'fōōs).
- Kugler (kōōg'lẽr).
- Laud (la̤d).
- Lely (lē'lĭ).
- Lennox (Lĕn'nǫx).
- Louvre (lōō'vr).
- Lübke (lṳb'ke̤).
- Macaulay (mȧ-ka̤'lĭ).
- Madonna (Mȧdŏn'nȧ).
- Magdalene (Măg'dā-lēn).
- Masaccio (mä-sät'chō).
- Médicis, Marie de (mä-rē' dẽ mā-dḗ-sēs').
- Metamorphoses (Mĕtȧmôr'phōsē̤s).
- Michelangelo (mē-kĕl-än'jā-lō).
- Minos (Mī'nŏs).
- Naseby (nāz'bĭ).
- Netherlands (nĕth'ẽr-lȧndz).
- Newcastle (nū'kȧsl).
- Nicodemus (nĭk-ō-dē'mŭs).
- Nood Godes (nōt gō'dĕs).
- Notre Dame (nō'tr däm).
- Ober-Ammergau (ō'bẽr äm'mẽrgow).
- Ovid (ŏv'ĭd).
- Padua (Păd'ūȧ).

- Palatine (păl'a̍-tīn).
- Palermo (På lẽr'mō).
- Paradise (Păr'a̍dīse).
- Parliamentarians (pär-lĭ-měn-tā'rī-a̍nz).
- Pellegrino, Monte (mōn'tā̄ pĕl-lā̄-grē'-nō).
- Pesaro (pā-sä'rō).
- Peveril (Pĕv'e̱r̃ĭl).
- Phillips, Claude (kla̱d fil'ĭps).
- Pietà (pē ā̄ tä').
- Plantin (pläN-tăN).
- Pontius Pilate (pŏn'shĭ-ŭs pī'lā̄t).
- Portuguese (pōr'tū-gēz).
- Puritans (pū'rĭ-ta̍nz).
- Raphael (rä'fā-ĕl).
- Reynolds (rĕn'o̱lz).
- Richardot, Jean Grusset (zhäN gru̱s-sā' rē-shär-dō').
- Richmond (Rĭch'mo̱nd).
- Rosalia (rō-zā'lĭ-a̍).
- Rubens (r$\overline{oo}$ 'běnz).
- Rupert (r$\overline{oo}$ 'pe̱rt).
- Ruthven (Rūth'věn).
- Samothrace (săm'ō̇-thrās).
- Scone (sk$\overline{oo}$ n).
- Sheffield (shĕf'ēld).
- Sicilians (sĭ-sĭl'ĭ-a̍nz or sĭ-sĭl'ya̍nz).
- Sicily (sĭs'ĭ-lĭ).
- Strickland (Strĭck'la̍nd).

- Stuart (Stū'ȧrt).
- Thames (tĕmz).
- Titian (tĭsh'ȧn).
- Toulouse (t$\overline{oo}$-l$\overline{oo}$ z').
- Tours (t$\overline{oo}$ r).
- Vän Bălĕn.
- Van der Geest (vän där gāst).
- Van Dyck (văn dīk).
- Vatican (văt'ĭ kȧn).
- Vaughn (vạṇ).
- Venetian (vé-nē'shȧn).
- von Ranke (fṓn rän'keˌ).
- Wake (wāk).
- Wandesford, Rowland (wŏnz'foṛd rō'lȧnd).
- Warwick (waṛ'ĭk).
- Wentworth (Wĕnt'woṛth).
- Wharton (Whaṛ'toṇ).
- Winchendon (Wĭn'chĕndoṇ).
- Windsor (wĭn'zoṛ).
- Woerman (w$\overline{oo}$ r'män).
- Woltman (Wŏlt'män).
- Zebedee (Zĕb'ĕdēē).
- Zeus (zūs).

Milton Keynes UK
Ingram Content Group UK Ltd.
UKHW030743071024
449371UK00006B/602